Saltwater Crocodiles

Nature's Biggest Reptile

Jackie Golusky

Lerner Publications • Minneapolis

Lerner Publications Company
An imprint of Lerner Publishing Group, Inc.
241 First Avenue North
Minneapolis, MN 55401 USA

For reading levels and more information, look up this title at www.lernerbooks.com.

Main body text set in Billy Infant Regular. Typeface provided by SparkType.

Editor: Annie Zheng **Photo Editor:** Annie Zheng

Library of Congress Cataloging-in-Publication Data

Names: Golusky, Jackie, 1996- author.
Title: Saltwater crocodiles : nature's biggest reptile / Jackie Golusky.
Description: Minneapolis : Lerner Publications, [2024] | Series: Lightning Bolt Books. Nature's most massive animals | Includes bibliographical references and index. | Audience: Ages 6-9 | Audience: Grades 2-3 | Summary: "What are the most massive reptiles on the planet? Saltwater crocodiles! In this book, young readers will learn about where they live, what they eat, and how they're cared for when they're born"— Provided by publisher.
Identifiers: LCCN 2023006987 (print) | LCCN 2023006988 (ebook) | ISBN 9798765608449 (lib. bdg.) | ISBN 9798765615508 (epub)
Subjects: LCSH: Crocodylus porosus—Juvenile literature. | BISAC: JUVENILE NONFICTION / Animals / Reptiles & Amphibians
Classification: LCC QL666.C925 G665 2024 (print) | LCC QL666.C925 (ebook) | DDC 597.98/2—dc23/eng/20230320

LC record available at https://lccn.loc.gov/2023006987
LC ebook record available at https://lccn.loc.gov/2023006988

ISBN 979-8-7656-2433-3 (pbk.)

Manufactured in the United States of America
1-1009289-51498-5/23/2023

Table of Contents

Sneaky Hunters

A saltwater crocodile hides in the water. Only its eyes and nose can be seen above the surface. It spots a snake in the trees. It prepares to lunge.

Saltwater crocodiles are the world's biggest reptile. A reptile is a cold-blooded animal. Reptiles generally lay eggs and have a body covered in scales or hard parts.

A saltwater crocodile

Growing Up

Between November and May, a female saltwater crocodile prepares her nest. She lays about forty to sixty eggs.

When the baby crocodiles are ready to hatch, they call for their mother. The mother digs up the eggs and puts them in her mouth. She carefully bites down to help the babies hatch.

Saltwater crocodile eggs hatch after about ninety days.

Baby saltwater crocodiles are called hatchlings. They are about 11 inches (28 cm) long and weigh about 2.5 ounces (72 g).

Baby saltwater crocodiles

Hatchlings eat insects, crabs, frogs, and small fish. As they get bigger, they can eat turtles, snakes, birds, and even buffalo.

A hatchling near a river in Australia

Off the Coasts

Saltwater crocodiles live in eastern India, Southeast Asia, and northern Australia. They can be found on ocean coasts or in freshwater swamps.

A saltwater crocodile warms up in the sun.

Since they are cold-blooded, their bodies can get too cold or too hot. Crocodiles will lie out in the sun to stay warm. Or they will cool off in the water.

Adult saltwater crocodiles usually live alone. Male saltwater crocodiles are territorial and will drive away other male crocodiles.

Saltwater crocodiles fighting

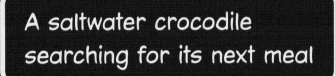

A saltwater crocodile searching for its next meal

These crocodiles are carnivores. They eat other animals. Saltwater crocodiles tend to hunt at night.

Life of a Crocodile

Saltwater crocodile hatchlings will be female if the temperature in their nest is cooler. In warmer temperatures, hatchlings will be male.

After the eggs hatch, the mother carries them to the water. She will stay with the young crocodiles for several months. Then they will be on their own.

A hatchling rides on top of its mother's head.

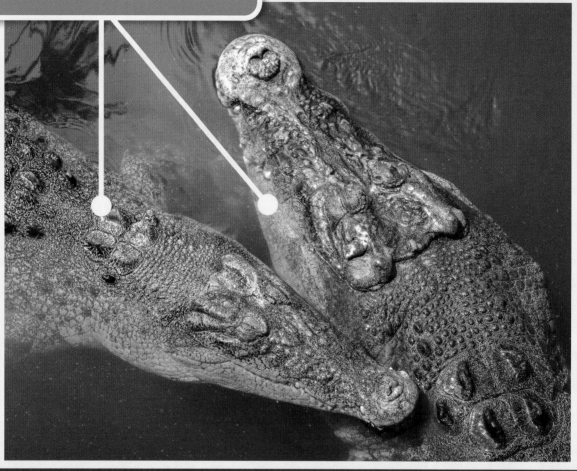

Left to right: a female and a male crocodile

Female saltwater crocodiles are fully grown at ten to twelve years old. They can grow up to 10 feet (3 m) and weigh up to 330 pounds (150 kg).

A large male saltwater crocodile in shallow water

Male crocodiles are fully grown at sixteen years old. They can grow up to 23 feet (7 m) and weigh more than 2,200 pounds (1,000 kg).

Climate change is causing temperatures to rise. Warmer temperatures mean fewer female saltwater crocodiles will hatch. This could make it harder for crocodiles to have babies.

A saltwater crocodile underwater

Saltwater crocodiles can live to be more than seventy years old. In that time, they will hunt, swim, and have babies of their own.

A group of saltwater crocodiles floats on the water's surface.

Saltwater Crocodile Diagram

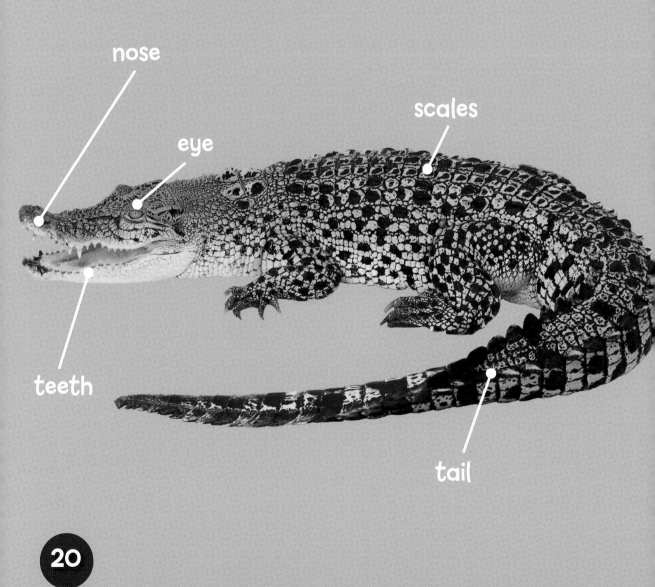

nose

eye

scales

teeth

tail

Fun Facts

- Saltwater crocodiles have sixty-six sharp teeth.

- Saltwater crocodiles communicate with one another by making different sounds. They can bark, hiss, growl, and chirp.

- Saltwater crocodiles can sleep with one eye open.

Glossary

climate change: significant, long-lasting change in Earth's climate and weather due to global warming

coast: the land along or near a sea or ocean

freshwater: water that is not salty

nest: a place or structure where eggs are laid and hatched

scale: a small, hard plate that covers animals such as snakes, alligators, and crocodiles

swamp: land that is always wet and often partly covered with water

temperature: how hot or cold something is

territorial: to act defensive over an area of land

Learn More

Animal Fun Facts: Saltwater Crocodile
https://www.animalfunfacts.net/crocodiles
/46-saltwater-crocodile.html

Britannica Kids: Crocodile
https://kids.britannica.com/kids/article
/crocodile/354338

Emminizer, Theresa. *Does Climate Change Affect Ecosystems?* New York: Enslow, 2023.

Golusky, Jackie. *Komodo Dragons: Nature's Biggest Lizard.* Minneapolis: Lerner Publications, 2024.

Murray, Julie. *Saltwater Crocodile.* Minneapolis: Dash!, 2021.

NASA Climate Kids: A Guide to Climate Change for Kids
https://climatekids.nasa.gov/kids-guide-to-climate
-change/

Index

Photo Acknowledgments

Image credits: Craig P. Jewell/Moment/Getty Images, p. 4; Uckarintra Wongcharit/Shutterstock, p. 5; Dody Karyanto/iStock/Getty Images, pp. 6, 7, 14; Supermop/Shutterstock, p. 8; Jamie Lamb/Moment/Getty Images, p. 9; Wirestock/iStock/Getty Images, p. 10; Dmitrii Mozhzherin/Shutterstock, p. 11; Max shen/Moment/Getty Images, p. 12; Kev Joyce/Alamy Stock Photo, p. 13; Xinhua/Alamy Stock Photo, p. 15; CMH Images/Alamy Stock Photo, p. 16; rweisswald/iStock/Getty Images, p. 17; Bernard Radvaner/Corbis/Getty Images, p. 18; Jason Edwards/Photodisc/Getty Images, p. 19; dwi putra stock/Shutterstock, p. 20.

Cover: ePhotocorp/iStock/Getty Images.